NATURE'S WRATH:

Surviving
Natural
Disasters

Survivors: Ordinary People, Extaordinary Circumstances

An Enemy Within:
Overcoming Cancer and Other Life-Threatening Diseases

Danger in the Deep:
Surviving Shark Attacks

Gender Danger:
Survivors of Rape, Human Trafficking, and Honor Killings

In Defense of Our Country:
Survivors of Military Conflict

Lost!
Surviving in the Wilderness

Nature's Wrath:
Surviving Natural Disasters

Never Again:
Survivors of the Holocaust

Students in Danger:
Survivors of School Violence

Survival Skills:
How to Handle Life's Catastrophes

Those Who Remain:
What It Means to Be a Survivor

We Shall All Be Free:
Survivors of Racism

When Danger Hits Home:
Survivors of Domestic Violence

The World Gone Mad:
Surviving Acts of Terrorism

NATURE'S WRATH:

Surviving Natural Disasters

Ellyn Sanna

 Mason Crest Publishers

NATURE'S WRATH: Surviving Natural Disasters

MASON CREST PUBLISHERS INC.
370 Reed Road
Broomall, Pennsylvania 19008
(866)MCP-BOOK (toll free)
www.masoncrest.com

Because the stories in this series are told by real people, in some cases names have been changed to protect the privacy of the individuals.

Portions of this book originally appeared in *The Gift of Hope: In the Wake of the 2004 Tsunami and the 2005 Hurricanes* by Ellyn Sanna, 2006, and in *You and the Environment* by Rae Simons. Used with permission of Village Earth Books and AlphaHouse Publishing.

First Printing
9 8 7 6 5 4 3 2 1
ISBN 978-1-4222-0449-8 (series)
ISBN 978-1-4222-1462-6 (series)(pbk.)

    Library of Congress Cataloging-in-Publication Data
Sanna, Ellyn, 1957–
  Nature's wrath : surviving natural disasters / by Ellyn Sanna.
      p. cm. — (Survivors--ordinary people, extraordinary circumstances)
  Includes bibliographical references.
  ISBN 978-1-4222-0454-2   ISBN 978-1-4222-1467-1
  1. Natural disasters—Juvenile literature. I. Title.
GB5019.S27 2009
363.34—dc22
                                        2008033334

Design by MK Bassett-Harvey.
Produced by Harding House Publishing Service, Inc.
www.hardinghousepages.com
Cover design by Wendy Arakawa.
Printed in The Hashimite Kingdom of Jordan.

CONTENTS

Introduction

Each of us is confronted with challenges and hardships in our daily lives. Some of us, however, have faced extraordinary challenges and severe adversity. Those who have lived—and often thrived—through affliction, illness, pain, tragedy, cruelty, fear, and even near-death experiences are known as survivors. We have much to learn from survivors and much to admire.

Survivors fascinate us. Notice how many books, movies, and television shows focus on individuals facing—and overcoming—extreme situations. *Robinson Crusoe* is probably the earliest example of this, followed by books like the *Swiss Family Robinson*. Even the old comedy *Gilligan's Island* appealed to this fascination, and today we have everything from the Tom Hanks' movie *Castaway* to the hit reality show *Survivor* and the popular TV show *Lost*.

What is it about survivors that appeals so much to us? Perhaps it's the message of hope they give us. These people have endured extreme challenges—and they've overcome them. They're ordinary people who faced extraordinary situations. And if they can do it, just maybe we can too.

This message is an appropriate one for young adults. After all, adolescence is a time of daily challenges. Change is everywhere in their lives, demanding that they adapt and cope with a constantly shifting reality. Their bodies change in response to increasing levels of sex hormones; their thinking processes change as their brains develop, allowing them to think in more abstract ways; their social lives change as new people and peers become more important. Suddenly, they experience the burning need to form their own identities. At the same time, their emotions are labile and unpredictable. The people they were as children may seem to have disappeared beneath the onslaught of new emotions, thoughts, and sensations. Young adults have to deal with every single one of these changes, all at the same time. Like many of the survivors whose stories are told in this series, adolescents' reality is often a frightening, confusing, and unfamiliar place.

Young adults are in crises that are no less real simply because these are crises we all live through (and most of us survive!) Like all survivors, young adults emerge from their crises transformed; they are not the people they were before. Many of them bear scars they will carry with them for life—and yet these scars can be integrated into their new identities. Scars may even become sources of strength.

In this book series, young adults will have opportunities to learn from individuals faced with tremendous struggles. Each individual has her own story, her own set of circumstances and challenges, and her own way of coping and surviving. Whether facing cancer or abuse, terrorism or natural disaster, genocide or school violence, all the survivors who tell their stories in this series have found the ability and will to carry on despite the trauma. They cope, persevere, persist, and live on as a person changed forever by the ordeal and suffering they endured. They offer hope and wisdom to young adults: if these people can do it, so can they!

These books offer a broad perspective on life and its challenges. They will allow young readers to become more self-aware of the demanding and difficult situations in their own lives—while at the same time becoming more compassionate toward those who have gone through the unthinkable traumas that occur in our world.

— Andrew M. Kleiman, M.D.

Chapter One

OUR RELATIONSHIP WITH PLANET EARTH

Once upon a time, human beings thought of the planet where they lived as their mother. They knew all life came from the Earth, that they were dependent on her bounty. They appreciated her and loved her, they worked to understand her better and live at peace with her. As every mother's child knows, mothers can lose their tempers, and as the saying goes, "If Mama ain't happy, ain't no one happy!" An unhappy mother cannot nurture her family—but a mother who is cherished and loved is much easier to get along with than one who is neglected and taken for granted.

In the long-ago world where human children loved Mother Earth, people left few scars on the land. They followed the natural sequence of the seasons; they were hunters and gatherers

We think
of Earth as
something
stable and
solid—but in
reality, the
Earth has
always been
part of a living
and turbulent
system of
natural forces.

The Earth may have once been thought of as a well-loved mother—but she was also respected. Human beings have always known that the same Earth that feeds us and gives us life can also turn deadly. The immense natural forces that first shaped our planet more than 4 billion years ago continue to be at work, both beneath the Earth's crust and millions of miles out in space. The sun's energy continues to impact our planet, while the Earth's own crust shifts, creating cracks into the molten core. As a result, our planet has always endured blizzards and floods, windstorms and lava flows, droughts and earthquakes. As *Life* author Ronald Boyer wrote, "We can call it nature's fury, but it is really nature's way."

who lived from the land in ancient ways that were similar to the animals'. But times changed. Agriculture—the art of farming—meant that people settled down in one place and began to shape the Earth to their own purposes. Slowly, gradually, the way they thought about their planet also began to change.

NEW THOUGHTS

Today we have words that put things into categories—terms like "natural world," "supernatural world," "manmade world"—and we think of these categories as being made up of separate things. A forest, a spirit, and a city are three different realities in our mental maps. But earlier thinkers looked at reality differently. They had no mental divisions between what was natural, what was

The long-ago people who created these cave drawings perceived reality as one connected "whole"—a world where nature, human life, and the spiritual world all intertwined.

supernatural, and what was human; it was all one thing. These long-ago human beings didn't even have the words to describe such a concept. There was just Everything: a living, breathing universe. People lived in a world where Earth, spirits, and human endeavors were intertwined, interdependent, indivisible.

It was the Greeks who first started looking at the world a little differently. The Greeks

were great **philosophers**; they studied the world and thought about it and came up with new words to describe it. The word that had once meant "Everything" was now divided: the concept of the spiritual or the supernatural came into existence, a reality separate from the "natural." In a similar way, human beings themselves were divided into two pieces as well: their minds/spirits were separate from their physical bodies. This

philosophers: people who search for wisdom and knowledge; thinkers.

Plato was an ancient Greek philosopher whose thinking continues to shape our world today.

way of thinking is called dualism; it means that we tend to look at the world in terms of two parts. And not only was the world made up of two parts—the physical/natural and the spiritual/supernatural—but the concept of "good" became tied to the spiritual world, while "bad" was associated with the physical world.

This kind of thinking wasn't necessarily worse than the old way of thinking—primitive cultures weren't all good, while modern cultures are all bad—but it was different. It meant that as people's perceptions of the world began to change, the world itself changed as well. For one thing, if the spiritual world is "good," it's worth more than the natural world; it deserves our attention and care. And if the natural world is "bad," that means we need to try to rise above it; as a result, we don't need to pay attention to it or take care of it. How do you think this affected the way people thought about the Earth?

> ## Thinkers Who Shaped the Modern World
>
> Plato and Aristotle were two of the ancient Greek world's greatest philosophers, and much of today's ideas about reality have their roots way back in the minds of these two great thinkers.

THE MAN-MADE WORLD

Ever since the beginning of human life, human beings have worked hard to protect themselves from the dangers of "nature." They built more efficient houses to guard

Aristotle was a student of Plato. He wrote down his teacher's ideas, preserving them so that they can still be read in the twenty-first century.

themselves against extremes in the weather; they invented a variety of weapons to protect them from wild animal attacks; they created medicines to ward off diseases; and they learned new ways to grow, store, and ship foods to prevent food shortages. Laborsaving inventions meant that fewer people could do all this more quickly and easily, so that the entire society no longer had to concern itself with the basic needs of survival. This meant that people like Plato and Aristotle actually had time to think, rather than spending their lives hunting and gathering food—and it meant that modern humans could create art and music, books and sports, television and computers, an entire fascinating culture that continues to evolve and grow.

As cities grew bigger, new inventions were made, and the world seemed so much

Kinds of Natural Disasters

Some scientist divide natural disasters into three categories: geological, hydrological, and climatic. Here are examples of each category:

Geological	Hydrological	Climatic
avalanche	flood	blizzard
earthquake	tidal wave/tsunami	hailstorm
landslide		drought
volcanic eruption		heat wave
		cyclonic storm (hurricanes, tornadoes, typhoons)

safer, human beings no longer *seemed* to be so dependent on Mother Earth's moods. After all, if you're living in a tent, a rainstorm is a big deal, but if you're living in a skyscraper, you may barely notice it. Eventually, when bread and meat, Poptarts and Hamburger Helper all came wrapped in cardboard and

The residents of this house probably took their safety for granted—until a tornado destroyed their home.

plastic in the grocery store, many people found it difficult to remember that food actually still came from warm and breathing animal flesh or that it grew from green leaves and roots in brown dirt. Nature was a faraway concept, something to be appreciated on a hike through a park or on a camping

History's Natural Disasters

Ninety-nine entire families lost their lives in the Johnstown Flood of 1889 in Pennsylvania. There were survivors: ninety-eight children survived but lost their parents in the flood.

The 1902 volcanic eruption on the Caribbean island of Martinique killed an entire city of 30,000 people. There were only three survivors: a prisoner in an underground cell (who was eventually pardoned for his crime, since he had been through enough at that point!), a man who lived on the outskirts of the city, and a young girl.

The 1906 earthquake in San Francisco not only destroyed property and lives but also triggered fires from damaged electrical wires and overturned stoves. As many as 3,000 people were killed, and tens of thousands of survivors were left homeless. The city's recovery was long and difficult, much like New Orleans' is today after Hurricane Katrina.

The American Plains' Dust Bowl of the 1930s was caused in part by human activity: farmers had plowed and planted, plowed and planted, with no thought given to preserving topsoil. When a drought came, the soil simply blew away in the wind, causing "black blizzards" that reached as far East as Boston and New York City. The survivors—farmers whose land was no longer good for anything—took to the road in the largest migration in American history. The fact that the Great Depression was also going on didn't help their situation; they faced severe poverty and even starvation.

trip away from normal life. The "natural" and the "manmade" were now two separate things as well. People tended to forget how much they still relied on Planet Earth for their well-being.

Natural disasters, however, have a way of reminding us. When a flood or an earthquake disrupts our lives, suddenly the Earth becomes very real to us. Under these circumstances, though, we don't think of Nature as a warm, nurturing mother. Instead, we see it as something dangerous, unpredictable, and frightening. Nature is the enemy. We long to get back to "normal" life, the way it was before our house flooded or before the volcano erupted.

This photograph shows the damage to Johnstown's Main Street after the devastating 1889 flood.

In 1906, an earthquake left San Francisco in ruins.

The Dust Bowl was a natural disaster that went on and on for years. Entire farms were engulfed and destroyed by enormous clouds of dust.

Entire generations of children have grown up in the midst of Ethiopia's ongoing natural disaster. The deadly effects of drought have become a way of life.

Disasters That Never End

The people of Ethiopia and other African countries have been facing a series of natural disasters—droughts—that began in 1973 and show no sign of coming to an end. The drought of 1973 killed 300,000 people; the 1984–85 drought killed a million; and the cycle keeps occurring more and more frequently. (African droughts once occurred regularly every ten to fifteen years, but now they are coming every three years—and the cycle may become even shorter.) Some scientists blame El Niño (a periodic temperature increase in the Pacific Ocean), but others say that air pollution from Western countries is driving Africa's rain belt further south, allowing the Sahara's desert to encroach southward.

For some natural disaster survivors, however, there is no going back. Sometimes, as is the case for many of the survivors of Hurricane Katrina and the 2004 Asian tsunami, communities have been permanently destroyed; the survivors can never go home. On the island of Montserrat, a volcano that has been active for more than twelve years means that the crisis is ongoing, a fact of life with which the island's residents must live. In situations like these, survivors can no longer pretend that the Earth and its events don't matter. These people are faced with building with a "new normal."

Chapter Two

WHEN THE OCEAN OVER-FLOWS: *TSUNAMI SURVIVORS*

Imagine a hot summer's day. You and your family are vacationing at the beach, and it's one of those lazy, sunny days where everyone is relaxed, everyone is happy. Suddenly, you notice something strange: something is sucking the water away from the beach, pulling it further and further away, leaving a long expanse of wet sand littered with shells and sea creatures. Curious, you run after the retreating water.

You don't know that miles away, in the center of the ocean, an immense earthquake has shaken the foundations of the sea, triggering a monstrous wave. You certainly never suspect that the sunny summer day that seems so innocent will turn out to be deadly.

But when you see an immense wall of water speeding toward you, you begin to run.

When the 2004 tsunami swept onto land, people ran frantically for safety, while others stood stunned. Thousands died.

BOONSRUONG'S STORY

The year 2004 was a hard one for Boonsruong Dheva-aksorn. The death of her beloved grandfather, combined with a series of health problems, had left her emotionally and physically drained. A Christmas holiday with her husband and ten-year-old son at the resort of Phang-Nga in Thailand was exactly what she needed to restore her spirits.

On the morning of December 26, Boonsruong rested in their hotel room while her husband and son enjoyed a swim. Then she heard shouts and screams, and her husband

Boonsruong with her husband and son.

What Is Dharma?

Dharma is a Buddhist concept that describes the underlying order in nature and life. It is the harmony that upholds the world. Peace and happiness in this world are achieved by following the practices of dharma.

and son burst into the room. Before she could realize what was happening, torrents of ocean water ripped through the front wall of the room.

At first, the family swirled around and around within the room's walls; then all four walls collapsed and the water's suction tore them apart from each other. Buried beneath a mountain of water, Boonsruong struggled to hold her breath. "This is your last breath," she told herself. "Hold it. Hold it for an eternity. If you let go of this last breath, you will be dead." Her desperate thoughts turned into a prayer. In the midst of the water, she asked for the grace and blessing of Buddha and Dharma.

Finally, after being swept more than three hundred feet from the hotel, she grabbed a tree trunk and pulled her head above the water. She sucked in a breath and clung, bleeding, exhausted, waiting for the water to recede.

"Buddha teaches that one is one's own refuge," Boonsruong said. "In the midst of destruction, surrounded by debris, [you can]

Who Is Buddha?

Siddhartha Gautama was a spiritual teacher from ancient India (somewhere between 563 and 483 BCE), who founded the religion of Buddhism and became known as the Buddha. Some Buddhists believe he was a human being who was extremely wise and was able to achieve a degree of enlightenment that few if any other humans have reached. Other Buddhists, however, believe he is an eternal being, the ultimate expression of all that is real and true.

find yourself, even as you discard all else." This is what she experienced as she struggled for life in the midst of the tsunami's wave. As her senses returned to her, she looked down and realized her clothes had been swept away by the water, leaving her naked. Strange, detached thoughts flickered through her mind: "Naked I was born into this world. When I die, I will be truly naked, for I will have discarded even my own body. Perhaps I am already dead, buried beneath the massive wave. But now I am reborn, naked, just as I was born the first time." For a moment, joy swept through her, followed quickly by fear and sorrow for her family.

An hour later, to her great joy, she and her husband and son were reunited. "We were like cockroaches caught in a toilet bowl," her son said. "Whirling in circles in the water."

As a good Buddhist, Boonsruong never killed the cockroaches she found in their home; instead, she put them in the toilet. "You will not die," she would tell them. "For

A beachfront resort home once stood here on the coast of Thailand. The 2004 tsunami washed away everything but the foundation and the toilet base.

Why Won't a Buddhist Kill a Cockroach?

Buddhists believe in nonviolence and compassion—and they extend this to even the lowest life forms, including insects, since all life is holy, full of meaning and value. Although human beings sometimes cannot help but kill insects unintentionally, no violence should be committed intentionally.

the time being, gyrating in the toilet bowl may be a bit of a torture—but soon you will be safe in another place." Boonsruong smiled through her tears. She and her family were in a very different place than the one where they had been when they'd woken up that morning on vacation—but at least they were safe.

PRASIT'S STORY

The morning of Sunday, December 26, 2004, dawned clear and serene. Prasit Sathaphonchaturawit, the director of the Bangsak School in Thailand's Phang-Nga Province, woke early, just as he always did, and stepped outside to breathe the air. With a sense of contentment, he ate his breakfast and then drove to the school. The sun glimmered through the trees off the ocean as he got out of his car.

Prasit smiled as he walked down the school's empty corridor and went into his office. His life pleased him: there was his desk, piled with work; his office walls were

Prasit points to the tree where he was swept by the tsunami's force.

hung with pictures of students' activities to encourage him with the reason for his work; and contest certificates and sport trophies reminded him of his school's successes. Prasit sat down at his desk; by noon, he hoped to have made his way through at least half the stack of papers.

But his concentration was disturbed by shouts outside the school building. The voices

grew louder, and Prasit got up to look out the window. Streaming past the school was a jittery mass of human beings, climbing as fast as they could toward higher land. With a sense of unreality, he heard them screaming for their children, crying for help, sobbing.

And then Prasit turned his gaze in the opposite direction, toward the trees through which he normally glimpsed the shining

This child lost his father in the tsunami—but Prasit's rebuilt school offers him both a home and a place to learn.

ocean. Instead, he saw a wall of water taller than the trees. Without further thought, he rushed to his car.

Too late. The water had already heaved his car into the air. A breath later, it snatched Prasit and threw him upward, like an enormous hand tossing a ball. As the school disappeared beneath the immense wave, a tall, deeply rooted tree caught Prasit in its branches. A few minutes later, his desk chair landed on the branch beside him.

Prasit found himself surveying a nightmare. Below him was a wide sea strewn with mangled cars pushed up against the ruined walls of his school. The Thai flag still fluttered from a flagpole, but everything else was gone.

Two more enormous waves surged around Prasit's tree—and then, just as suddenly as it had come, the water sucked backward. "I felt as though I had popped through a hole from one reality into another," Prasit said. When he climbed down his tree, the new reality he found was the most awful thing he had ever seen. Everywhere he looked, dead bodies were scattered in the mud and debris. His entire world had been washed away. He stood silent, shaking, staring, and thanked God that no students or teachers had been in the school.

But thirty-eight members of Prasit's family died that day.

The next day, Prasit was back at the school site. People were searching through the debris, seeking their loved ones, sunbathers and beachcombers who had been caught by the tsunami and washed up on the school grounds. He knew that many of his students had lost their lives; some had lost their parents; still others had lost their homes, their security, their families' livelihoods.

And yet life must go on, Prasit told himself. He could not stand grieving over the tragedy; if he did, he would give the disaster more destructive power than it **merited**. Instead, he said, "I renewed my commitment to the school."

merited: deserved; earned.

With the help of the school staff, Prasit gathered the remaining students and set up classrooms in the garage and backyard of a teacher's house. The same place soon became a relief center for the students' families who had been affected by the tsunami. Prasit realized he was not alone in his commitment; support poured in from across Thailand. And when the king of Thailand stepped in with help, Prasit said, "I knew a new day was dawning for my school. With His Majesty's help, Bangsak School, now Rajaprajanugroh 35th School, will become a warm shelter, a **sanctuary** for those who are waiting for a brighter day.

sanctuary: a safe place; a place of protection.

"I vow," said Prasit, "to spend the rest of my life helping my students cross the bridge that will carry them over the destructive waters, so that they can walk with grace toward a life of success and meaning. . . . Loving, caring, sharing, giving: these are the words that give our lives meaning here at Rajaprajanugroh 35th."

THE TAXI DRIVER'S STORY

"You just do the best you can," said a taxi driver in Phuket, Thailand. He handed his one-year-old son a toy, and then swung out around a slow-moving truck laden with passengers. The little boy pulled himself to his feet and peeked over the front seat at his father's passengers. The baby swung his plastic keys back and forth, chuckling, then ducked down and buried his face against

his father's arm. "I can't leave him while I work," his father explained. "I can't afford to pay someone to watch him."

"Where is his mother?"

"She was at the beach," the taxi driver said. "She died." The child fussed, and his father made a shushing noise, then tossed a single word over his shoulder: "Tsunami." The word is the same in Thai as in English.

The child continued to complain, and the driver abruptly pulled the taxi onto the road's shoulder. Without any explanation, he jumped out and ran around to the trunk; a moment later, he returned with a bottle of milk. The little boy plugged his mouth with the nipple and fell silent.

His father shrugged. "You just do what you have to do. The tsunami took away all our other choices."

But even in the strange, empty place left behind after the tsunami, survivors find ways to rebuild, to choose life. "In the place where you have no more choices," Solada Boonmee, another tsunami survivor, said, "where you can no longer evade your destiny, you have the opportunity to discover yourself."

NOY'S STORY

Noy is a woman who lives off the coast of Thailand on a tiny island. She is a member of a sea gypsy community that has endured for centuries. But on December 26, 2004, Noy's village changed forever.

Noy, a member of the Moken sea gypsy community, demonstrates a crab trap made by her family.

The Moken sea gypsies have lived on the Indian Ocean for as long as they remember. Once entire families spent their lives in long wooden boats, fishing with spears and nets, following the cycles of moon and **monsoon**. Their boats were their second bodies, the vessels that carried them through life, and the sea was their home, their element, as vital to their existence as the air they breathed. The Moken believed everything had a soul: the water, their boats, the trees and plants that grew on the islands, the wind and sky and sun. They had no concept of land ownership, no understanding of an economy based on money, and no **hierarchy** in their minds built on the words "rich" and "poor." Instead, their world was alive and friendly. Their connection to it was a simple fact of their daily lives.

But as the world changed, the Moken learned that if they kept to their ancient ways, spending only a few months on land, they soon had no place where they could return from the sea during the monsoons' storms. The islands in the Indian Ocean were a growing attraction for tourists from around the world, and the Moken could no longer assume their huts on stilts would be waiting for them when they came in from the sea.

hierarchy: a division or classification of society according to economic, social, or professional standing.

Moken Boats

The names for the parts of Moken boats are the same as the parts of the human body: *la-kae* (stomach), *ta-bin* (cheek), *tu-koh* (neck), *ba-hoy* (shoulder), and *ta-bing* (ribs). The Moken still feel the ancient vital connection between themselves and their kabang (boats). The well-being of a boat owner depends on the strength of the kabang; therefore, they build their boats from trees that are tall, straight, and smooth.

The ribbons tied around this Moken boat's prow honor the boat's spirit.

Squatters' rights:
the legal allowance to use a property because you are continuously living in it.

Squatters' rights were their only security, and many of the Moken moved into their land houses and settled down, fishing the waters near the islands by day but sleeping on dry land.

Gradually, the Moken adapted to contact with the rest of the world. They spoke their own language, but they learned other languages as well. They still ate mostly fish and the wild fruit and vegetables that grew on the islands, but now they also traded their fish for rice. Money had little place in their lives, Noy said. Coins and bills were for buying something pretty for a baby, a gold bracelet or a silver bangle. The sea and the land provided everything they truly needed.

They made their boats and knit their nets and fashioned traps for shrimp and crabs just as their ancestors had. But gasoline motors made their boats go faster, so that the men could follow the fish and get back home to their wives and children. And engines and gasoline cost money, which meant they now needed to catch enough fish and shrimp to sell to the tourist resorts—and still have enough left over to feed their families.

But still the men went out to sea and fished, while the women stayed behind to share the responsibilities of food preparation and child care. The young children played in the space between the huts, and the older ones went with their fathers to help with the catch. Houses were places for sleeping; the outdoors was where the community worked

Nong, Noy's husband, is at home in his boat as he is in his home. He navigates the water as though the boat were an extension of his body.

and talked and played. Food was everywhere, both on land and in the sea; garbage was nonexistent, because shells and husks degrade naturally; and the patterns of sun and moon, earth and sea were endlessly fascinating, more entertaining than any television drama. Their life was slow and simple and satisfying.

And then came the morning of December 26, 2004. With no money, no savings, no permanent possessions, the Moken were **vulnerable**. After the disaster, relief aid swept in from around the world, and the Moken were moved to temporary housing on the mainland. In effect, though, their lives were struck by two tsunamis: the first was a natural disaster caused by an earthquake deep below the ocean, but the second was a tidal wave of modern culture. Suddenly, they were exposed to a totally different way of living, a way that was built on cash and coins, on paper and plastic, on jobs and debt, bank accounts and possessions. "We learned we were poor," said Noy.

"Before the tsunami, we were like children," she said. "We didn't think about how we lived. We didn't pay attention to the choices we made. We just did what made us happy."

She pointed with pride to the wild orchids and other flowers she plants around her home, and she laughed as she described the culture shock she faced when the government moved the villagers to temporary housing

vulnerable: open to damage; weak.

on the mainland. (On one occasion, she and several other villagers were "trapped" in an elevator, not knowing they should push a button; another time, she nearly lost her **sarong** in a revolving door.)

"We couldn't stay on the mainland," she continued. "We don't belong there. We would stop being ourselves if we stayed. But since the tsunami, everything is different." She spoke slowly, giving the translator time to shape each word. "We have a chance to build ourselves something better—or we could lose everything. We have to think care-

sarong: a long strip of cloth that is wrapped around the body and worn as a skirt or dress by women and men.

A solar panel installed by the Thai government provides electricity to the thatched house that stands nearby.

After the tsunami, many islanders lived in housing like this provided by the government.

fully. We have to pay attention. The choices we make are important."

The Moken people on Noy's island did not lose their homes in the tsunami. Instead, they lost their boats. Forced to rent boats, their catch each month brought in barely enough money to cover their rent payments,

let alone to provide for their families. And at the same time, they were threatened with the loss of something even more valuable: their culture.

If you were to visit Noy's island, you would travel there in a small fishing boat that would carry you across the sea and into

A child on the island plants a tree, a symbol of the new life the islanders hope to build in the tsunami's wake.

the island's muddy channels. You would see fishing nets, small houses built on stilts, **mangroves** hung with spider webs. When you climbed on land, the villagers would watch you from the shadows beneath the trees. You might be impressed by how clean and American the children looked in their bright, new T-shirts emblazoned with Mickey Mouse and Cookie Monster. Their clothing had all been given to them after the tsunami, you'd learn, donations from people from around the world. You'd see piles of cardboard juice boxes outside the thatched houses, and heaps of plastic milk bottles scattered across the sand. (There is no trash collection on Noy's island, and no boat to carry it away if there were.) Small solar panels next to each home would seem **incongruous**, high-tech reminders of another world.

"The government installed them," Noy explained, "so that we can have electricity. So that we can have televisions—and if there is another tsunami, we will be able to hear the warning." She shrugged. "Now our children want to watch television instead of go to school. But if they do not go to school, the government will close the school. And if we have no school here, the government will send our children to a boarding school on the mainland." She shook her head. "We will not be separated from our children. But we cannot lose our life here on the island either. It is hard for people to see what needs to be done."

mangroves: coastal tropical trees or shrubs of the genus Rhizophora that send out dense masses of roots, which serve as unique and vital ecosystems; they are important in preventing coastal erosion and actually aid in rebuilding coastal land.

incongruous: inconsistent; mismatched.

What Is Malaria?

Malaria is a disease that's common in tropical and subtropical regions, including parts of the Americas, Asia, and Africa. Each year, about 515 million people will get malaria, and about 3 million of these will die. The disease is caused by tiny, single-celled parasites that are spread by mosquitoes. Symptoms of malaria include light-headedness, shortness of breath, fever, chills, and nausea.

Noy spoke at length of the way life had been before the tsunami, the closeness they had shared, the joy the sea had given them. When the tsunami came, many of the Moken villages were completely destroyed, and their residents now live in temporary government housing on the mainland. Noy's village, however, was far enough inland that the houses still stand. "The government wanted us to stay on the mainland," she said. "And some of us were afraid to come back. But us," she waved her hand around the ragged circle of houses, "we knew we had to come back, even if the government didn't want us to. If there is another tsunami, my husband and I will not leave again. If we give up our homes, we will give up our lives."

Before the tsunami, the Moken people, both in Myanmar and in Thailand, were in danger of losing their traditional homes to the onslaught of tourism. The islands along the coasts of Myanmar and Thailand were like bright jewels scattered across the turquoise water. From a practical, economic perspective, these islands are ripe for development.

The tsunami changed that. The once golden beaches are gone; what's left were ragged stumps and standing waters where malaria now breeds. But the tsunami has also brought the Moken to the world's attention. Their survival stories made international news, and **sociologists** from around the world are now studying their situation. Swamped by a tide of Western values, their culture is in danger of being submerged—but as Noy said, they also have the opportunity now to climb out of the flood and claim their own identity in a new way.

sociologists: scientists who study society, especially the development, structure, interaction, and collective behavior of organized groups of human beings.

Chapter Three

WHEN HOMES ARE SWEPT AWAY: *HURRICANE SURVIVORS*

North America is linked to the Atlantic Ocean by a mighty stream of water, the Mississippi River. The first Europeans who mapped the Mississippi and its wetlands called it a "gathering of waters"; it is also a gathering place for life, including human life. Native Americans viewed the great river as the center of their universe. They understood how vital its life was to their own economies. They used it for transportation; they ate from its table; they respected its power. Like the Moken, they had no concept of land ownership; instead, they lived in harmony with the Earth, dependent on its bounty.

From space, the Mississippi River Delta looks like a green tree, a living organism sprawled across North America.

Changing Perspectives

In the eighteenth century, the French settlers who moved into the wetlands along the Gulf Coast brought with them the concept of land ownership. They also learned much from the Indians, however, about how to live off this land. Fishermen and trappers, the French settlers formed their own unique culture that was dependent on the cycles of tide and seasons.

When the United States took possession of the Mississippi as part of the Louisiana Purchase, the riverbanks were soon flooded with white settlements, and the Native people—the Houma and the Chitamacha, the Bayougoula and all the others—were driven literally to land's end, to the very edge of land and water. Meanwhile, the settlers were busy: trees were cut, land drained, and sugarcane planted. Steamboats of the early nineteenth century pushed another wave of change across the Mississippi wetlands, as larger cities grew along the river.

commerce: the buying and selling of goods, involving transportation from place to place.

navigational: relating to the methods of determining position, course, and distance traveled in order to get ships or other vehicles from place to place.

levee: a built-up embankment meant to prevent flooding.

colonial: relating to the period of time when the Europeans living in North America still maintained ties with their parent countries.

The modern world's **commerce** and **navigational** demands brought **levee** construction and sandbar removals. Today the Mississippi's series of locks, dams, and levees creates a transportation corridor for the shipping industry. All these manmade changes made sense. After all, they helped make America rich. No one realized the importance of mud and marsh.

More than half of North America's wetlands have disappeared since **colonial** times, and at the mouth of the Mississippi River, nearly a thousand acres of land are lost each year. The state of Louisiana alone loses 25 to 35 square miles of wetlands a year. This means the United States is losing priceless resources—but it is also losing a natural flood-protection system that once absorbed storm water before it could harm low-lying communities.

Kerry St. Pé, director of the Barataria-Terrebonne National Estuary Program in southern Louisiana, remembers that once, back when he was a child, he would be excited when he heard a hurricane was approaching. Odds were good during hurricane season that a kid could get out of school for a few days of candlelight and special foods. "There was a

In the 1800s, riverboats chugged up and down the Mississippi River. No one considered the effect that commerce might have upon the river.

Nature's Way

Left to itself, nature maintained the marshlands. The river carried rich sediment that built up new land even as other land was flooded. Today, however, dams, artificial banks, and levees funnel the river straight into the Gulf—and silt flows with it, leaving behind eroded land that is sinking beneath the water.

level of excitement that **permeated** our whole culture," St. Pé says. "Now, I approach each hurricane season with a sense of dread."

permeated: spread through or filled.

Like the Moken in Thailand, the people who live in the wetlands of Louisiana and Mississippi are vulnerable. Those who lack savings and insurance, who are more dependent on the simple resources of community and nature, are most vulnerable of all. When hurricanes Katrina and Rita slammed the Gulf Coast, those who had the least in material goods were the least willing to leave their homes. They had nowhere else to go. "You have to accept," said Kirby Verret, a Houma Indian, "that normal's never going to be the same."

More than a year after Katrina, neat blue tarps covered missing roofs in the wealthier subdivisions outside New Orleans, where life was clearly continuing, slowly and painfully, despite the mess Katrina had left behind. In the Ninth Ward, though, only a ghost town remained: block after block of ruined houses,

Kirby Verret is a Houma leader as well as a Methodist minister.

flooded cars, and mud. In St. Bernard Parish, the highway traveled between miles and miles of swamped boats, stranded refrigerators and air conditioning units, broken signs, piles of plastic and boards and metal. Even in the midst of all this destruction, however, life continued.

TRAEMEL'S STORY

Before Hurricane Katrina, Traemel Day had plans for her life. She was going to get out of the Projects; she was going to save enough money to start her own catering business; she was going to make a better life for herself and her children. Traemel held down a full-time job, took care of her kids, and went to school at New Orleans' Culinary Institute. Book by book, she built up her collection of

Traemel Day admires her new home, provided to her by Habitat for Humanity.

recipes, knowing that her skill with flour and sugar, rolling pins and ovens, would one day be the foundation for her new life. By August 2005, she was only one course away from her culinary certification.

And then the hurricane hit New Orleans. The Culinary Institute was forced to close. The floodwaters ruined Traemel's collection of recipe books. Traemel and her family fled to Baton Rouge, leaving behind both their home and Traemel's plans for the future.

But with the help of the Baton Rouge Habitat for Humanity, Traemel and her children would have a new home, the first of the "homes in a box" that were built across the country. She got a new job as a security guard, and Traemel learned to hope again. "Katrina is like a love story," she said. "Sometimes it breaks your heart. But sometimes it makes you cry with joy, because you know out of the hardship a brighter future is being born— and there's going to be a happy ending after all. Things are gone in a wink of the eye. You can get angry. Or you can retrain your own mind. Reprogram your thoughts, like a soldier coming back from war. Teach yourself to see the opportunities. Make your eyes see hopeful things. Let it go and smile."

VALERIE'S STORY

Valerie Myles thought her happy ending had come years ago when she moved into her Habitat home. With a house of her own,

she could raise her children and build a life that made her proud. As the years went by, the promise of happiness was fulfilled, and when she got a cat, she named him Zion—after her church, where she had learned that the word Zion stood for a place of security and freedom.

Valerie with her cat Zion.

But then Katrina bore down on the Gulf Coast—and when Valerie fled her home, her cat had disappeared. She searched for him, called his name into the wind, and finally, was forced to leave without him. With tears on her face, she left behind her house, her Zion, and joined the exodus of people fleeing New Orleans. She feared she would see neither her home nor her cat again.

During her journey from the city, however, she heard a tiny voice crying—a scrawny pathetic kitten she adopted in Zion's place. She named the new cat Katrina, and she brought the little animal with her as she moved from one temporary home to another during the months she was away from home. For Valerie, the kitten was a symbol of hope, a gift the storm had given her.

Finally, two months later, she went home. Her house was wind damaged but not flooded, and to her great joy, she was able to move in again. Valerie showed the kitten Katrina her new home—and then, to her surprise, Valerie heard from beneath her porch a meow from another cat.

Zion picked his way across the debris-strewn yard and purred his greeting. His white coat was filthy; he was thin and ragged looking; but he had survived both Katrina and Rita.

"I've got my Katrina cat," Valerie said. "I've still got my house. And now I've got my Zion back."

BYRON AND SANDRA'S STORY

"The storm is one thing," Byron Winston said. "But it's the backside of the storm, what human beings do afterward, that's a bitter pill to swallow."

Byron, his wife Sandra, and their five children fled New Orleans when the waters started to rise around their home. "We didn't know what was happening," Sandra explained. "The electricity was off, so we couldn't listen to the radio. We didn't know the levees had broke."

Sandra describes the night when their lives fell apart. Byron was at the nursing home where he worked; Sandra sat all night by their door, a baseball bat clutched in her hands, afraid of the looters who ran through

Byron and Sandra live in an abandoned house while they wait for their new Habitat home.

What Is FEMA?

The Federal Emergency Management Agency—FEMA—is a part of the U.S. Department of Homeland Security, begun by Presidential Order on April 1, 1979. Its function is to coordinate disaster response efforts for all disasters that occur in the United States which overwhelm the local and state authorities. In order for FEMA to become involved, the governor of the state must declare a state of emergency and make a formal request to the President that FEMA become involved.

the dark streets. The next morning, Sandra and her children were able to make their way to Byron. With only a quarter of a tank of gas in their car, they joined the long line of traffic to Baton Rouge.

There they took shelter in an abandoned house. Friends gave them furniture. Their five children shared the two small bedrooms. "I cleaned," Sandra said. "Byron fixed things up."

The home they rented back in New Orleans was damaged beyond repair. "The landlords can't get help from FEMA for the repairs, because the properties aren't their residences," Byron explained. "And then what houses there are, we can't afford, not on my salary. Too much price gouging going on. Rents used to be $350; now they're $1200, $1500, $1700."

He shook his head. "So we live up here and I take the bus down to work. Four hours every day, coming and going, four hours

I don't have to be with my kids." He and his wife look at each other; this is clearly another conversation they've had before. "People don't think about how things are going to turn out down the road. I'm lucky, we're lucky. We got a place to stay, I got a job, we got food. But Sandra and I, we work hard to keep our kids good, to keep them off the streets. Now they don't hardly see their father. What's that going to do to them down the road, that's what I worry about. And what about families where both parents have to work to pay for the way things are now?

Trailers provided by FEMA stood empty for months after Hurricane Katrina, waiting for paperwork to be completed before the hurricane's refugees could inhabit them.

New Orleans'
Ninth Ward is
still recovering
from the
devastation left
by Hurricane
Katrina.

What about those kids who don't see either of their parents? Maybe they got a place to stay and food to eat, maybe they don't. But people aren't looking at what this storm could do to families."

"We all used to live together," Sandra said. "All our family, our parents, our brothers and sisters, all close by where we could help each other."

"Now we're scattered all over the country," Byron said. "Got family in Denver, in Florida, in Texas. The community's gone. We can't support each other. What's that going to do to us, to our children down the road? Who will we be?"

"Well, at least we'll have lots of places to visit," Sandra said.

Her husband smiled at her, but he shook his head. "You always see the bright side." He shrugged. "You're right, Sandra. But so am I."

Byron may be bitter—but as a hurricane survivor, he's also gained wisdom. "Tragedy you can't do nothing about. But now you gotta look for the silver lining. And that part's up to you." He added, "In the end, we're all on the same level, black and white, rich and poor. Just takes something like this to show what's what. After the hurricane, the beautifulest thing in the world happened: People walked around in each other's shoes."

Chapter Four

WHEN THE EARTH EXPLODES: *VOLCANO SURVIVORS*

In the middle of the Caribbean Sea, about 300 miles southeast of Puerto Rico, lies a tiny green island named Montserrat. At the beginning of the 1990s, it was a thriving British colony, a peaceful and prosperous community built mostly on tourism. Movie stars vacationed there, and the prestigious AIR Studios, built on the island by Beatles producer George Martin, recorded countless rock stars' albums. Millionaires had their villas on the island—including the owners of Mars Corporation (makers of Mars Bars and M&Ms), J.C. Penny, and Sprite—but Montserrat's real lifeblood was its ordinary people, descendents of freed slaves and Irish who came to escape religious persecution. The island's government had no debt, and the country was moving smoothly toward independence and self-sufficiency.

When
Montserrat's
volcano
exploded
in 1997, it
showered ash
on the capital
city of Plymouth.
Today, Plymouth
is buried deep
beneath layers
of volcanic
material.

But all the while, a fire slumbered deep below Montserrat's Soufriere Hills. In July 1995, it erupted—and it kept on erupting for years. The island's very shape was changed. Lives were lost, farmland destroyed, the harbor filled up with volcanic material, and the airport closed. The once prosperous community now relied on the United Kingdom for

Montserrat's History

When Christopher Columbus landed on the island in 1493, the Native Arawak and Carib people were living there. Columbus claimed the island for Spain and named it *Santa María de Montserrate* in honor of a monastery on Spain's Mountain of Montserrat. In 1632, the island fell under English control, and a group of Irish Catholics seeking religious freedom settled there. Slaves from West Africa were brought to the island, and the economy was built on the production of sugar, rum, arrowroot, and cotton. A failed slave uprising on March 17, 1798 led to St. Patrick's Day being declared a public holiday. Slavery was finally abolished on the island in 1834. Falling sugar prices during the nineteenth century hurt the island's economy, but new opportunities were born from this challenge. In 1869, Joseph Sturge of Birmingham, England, formed the Montserrat Company to buy failed sugar estates, which he transformed into lime plantations. The island became famous for its limejuice, and the Montserrat Company set up a school and sold parcels of land to the island's inhabitants, creating a community of small landowners.

The volcano has left barren inlets of ash across Montserrat's green and fertile land.

its survival, but a government far across the Atlantic could not always comprehend the real needs of Montserrat's survivors.

ARTHUR'S STORY

In 1997, two years after Montserrat's volcano first became active, Arthur Meade said he was "living on the flanks of the volcano." The words he used again and again to describe the volcano made it seem like a living beast, something large and dangerous, yet not completely unfriendly.

Arthur's life, he said, was a happy one: he worked at the airport, he loved his house, and the scientific community on Montserrat assured everyone that both the airport and the houses that clung to the mountain's side were safe. "We had a false sense of security," Arthur said. "We didn't realize that the government was pressuring the scientists to say we were safe. After all, by that point, the airport was the only way in and out of Montserrat."

What Causes Volcanoes?

A volcano is a break in the Earth's crust that allows molten rock, ash, and gas to escape from inside the Earth. As rock is pushed upward, these cracks tend to form mountains.

The illusion of safety couldn't last forever, though, no matter how much the local and British government might have hoped. The mountain erupted again, destroying the airport, houses, and nineteen human lives. Arthur was forced to abandon the home he had loved so much.

But one sunny day he went back to visit his old house. The familiar building seemed so normal, so much like it always had, that he couldn't believe he would never live there again. As he moved around the well-known rooms, however, he noticed that the light in the house was growing dim, though evening was still hours away.

Arthur Meade barely escaped the volcano's pyroclastic flow.

When he stuck his head out the door, he saw that ash was shooting 30 feet into the air from the mountaintop; it was so thick that it looked as though night were falling. By this time, though, after years of living with an active volcano, Arthur wasn't particularly worried. He was used to seeing the ash vents. It never occurred to him that his life was in danger.

A few minutes later, though, he noticed that the water in the ghaut (pronounced "gut," the word means a "deep gully") near his home was steaming. This was something Arthur had never seen happen before. He decided it was time for him to leave his old home.

By now the air was so thick with ash that he could barely see the road ahead as he

Arthur's foot and leg still show the scars left by his encounter with the volcano.

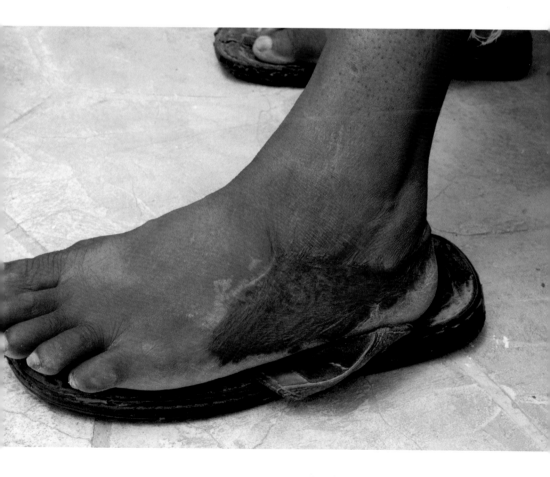

drove, even with his headlights shining. The air in the car was stifling; automatically, he clicked on the car's air conditioning, only to have scalding air sucked into the car's interior. Fire was all around the car now.

Arthur knew his car could not carry him to safety. He leapt out into the surge of **pyroclastic flow**. Feeling as though he had stumbled into Hell, he tried to make his way to safety—but he didn't know where safety lay, and the very air burned his throat.

pyroclastic flow:
a fast-moving flow of hot gas and rock, which can move away from the volcano at a speed greater than 50 mph and a temperature of 1,800°F.

"Arthur, why don't you bend?" According to Arthur, a small voice spoke to him in the midst of his fear. "Why don't you stoop?" When he bent over, he found he could breath. But the fire was burning up through his shoes; his socks burst into flame. "I was seeing the stars in heaven," he said.

He remembered he had left a flashlight in the car, and he managed to stumble back to retrieve it. It seemed like a **divine** gift that it was there for this moment of terrible need. By its light, he managed to make his way a short distance, but then the ash became too thick for the light to penetrate. "Arthur," said the voice in his head, "why don't you stoop again?"

divine:
relating to a god or God.

When he bent over, Arthur saw the line of green against gray, where the pavement met the grass on the road's shoulder. He followed that line of green, terrified all the while that he would be killed by one of the stones that tumbled down from the sky. The ten-minute walk into the village took him an hour, but

NO ENTRY
BEYOND THIS POINT

THIS AREA HAS BEEN DESIGNATED AN UNSAFE ZONE

ALL UNAUTHORISED ACCESS IS PROHIBITED AND ANY
UNAUTHORISED ENTRY IS SUBJECT TO PROSECUTION

at last, with his skin burned away from the bones of his feet, he reached safety.

An hour later, when the volcano fell silent once more, a friend took Arthur back to his car. Its engine was still running, but its rear tires had burned down to the metal rims. Arthur drove it out of the danger zone on only two tires. "The handiwork of the Almighty kept me alive," he said. "Otherwise I would have been a dead, dead, dead man."

An army helicopter flew Arthur off Montserrat, to a hospital on the island of Guadalupe, where his life became a cycle of surgeries and skin grafts. "I lost myself for

Residents of Montserrat can look across the fence that separates them from the land that was once their homes. Although the volcano has not engulfed all the island beyond this sign, the government has deemed it too close to the volcano to be safe.

awhile," he said, describing the days of anesthesia and **IV drips**.

Eventually, he was released from the hospital, and finally he came home. Today he considers himself a changed man. "The love of what you have is a **vanity**," he said. "You learn the love of just living is greater. You lose your sense of control when you live with a volcano."

A decade later, much of the island is still off limits, part of what the government has termed the "Exclusion Zone," the area most threatened by the volcano. The once -familiar streets and houses are now as unreachable as if they were on the moon. Arthur compares the **habitable** area where the community remains to a "comfort zone." He said, "People don't want to leave their comfort zones. But we have to be willing to look over the borderlands into the Exclusion Zone—both on the island and in our own heart—and see what's real. What's real is plenty of dirt and mess—but we can't be ashamed to confront the dirt."

Today, Arthur has a passion: to pick up all the debris and garbage from his island. "Before I close my eyes," he said, referring to his eventual death, "I want to see the island clean." His brush with death, a death that would have been dealt to him by the very island he loves so much, gave him a new love for this small piece of land. "The volcano lives with us," he said. "Now we have to learn to live with it."

SHIRLEY'S STORY

Shirley Spycalla and her husband Lou run one of the island's only remaining hotels, Erindell Villa Guesthouse, a small friendly place where Lou cooks the guests' food. Over the years, they've thought about leaving; after all, it's hard to run a guesthouse on an island that regularly runs out of gas, coffee, toilet paper, and beer. What's more, they're fed up with "the English"; you'd think you were back in Revolutionary America from the

Shirley and Lou Spycalla in front of Erindell, their guesthouse.

Despite its problems, Shirley loves her island home.

way these frustrated colonists talk. And yet, like Arthur Meade, Shirley loves the island. "There's so little crime here," she said. "No muggings, no break-and-entry. It's a close-knit community." She knows everyone by first name on the island, and she knows all the family stories.

And yet living on Montserrat, said Shirley, means living in a state of "ongoing crisis." She described what it was like to have your life interrupted over and over by the sound of the siren playing the Westminster chimes, alerting the community that the volcano was once again threatening it. "When you hear the loud speaker shouting, 'Ee-vack-you-ate! Ee-vack-you-ate!' you wonder, 'Where?' How are you supposed to know where to go to be safe?"

Ash masks and brooms are a part of daily life for Shirley. She knows what it's like to see burning stones fall on her roof, while glowing embers float through the sky like

Layers of ash everywhere are part of daily life on Montserrat.

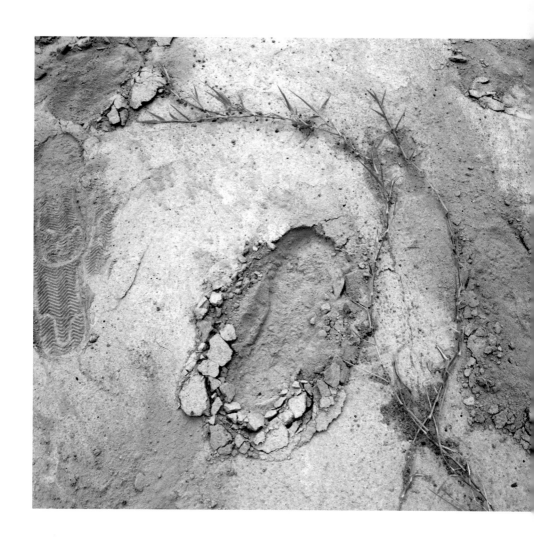

pumice:
a lightweight volcanic rock that is full of holes.

fireflies. Picking up **pumice** stones is a regular chore. In 2003, the volcano's ash fell from the sky mixed with rain. "It was a mudfall," Shirley said, "instead of a rainfall. It settled like concrete, six-feet deep." Three men— "angels with shovels," Shirley called them— showed up to help Shirley and Lou dig out their property from the heavy, ashy mud.

Shirley doesn't give up. She entertains her guests with her stories and her opera singing; she helps visitors see just how beautiful this island is. Along with her husband Lou, Shirley is sticking it out on Montserrat—and she's spreading the word that this island community is worth saving.

SARAH'S AND SIMORRA'S STORIES

Sarah and Simorra have lived most of their sixteen years with a volcano always in the background; they were four years old when Montserrat's volcano first became active. They remember how they felt: Sarah was thrilled and excited, while Simorra was scared.

Since then, their lives have been continually disrupted by the volcano: Simorra's family has moved ten times, while Sarah's has moved four or five times. Simorra lived in England for a year and a half, where one of her sharpest memories is of snow.

"You get used to moving all the time," Simorra said. "You just pick up your suitcase

Simorra and Sarah

and do it all again. Soon as you get comfortable one place, you have to move."

"At first," Sarah said, "you want to take everything. After a while, you start to realize you don't need all that much, and it's easier if you don't have so much. You learn that needs aren't the same thing as wants."

"You get so you appreciate the color green," Simorra put in, "when you grow up with everything being gray with ash so much of the time. The ashfall breaks the trees, clings to everything, even the flowers."

Before the volcano, Sarah's family ran a water-sports store that **catered** to tourists. "The volcano changed who I am," she said. "I would have grown up as a beach bum. I lost the sea."

"We had more friends before the volcano," said Simorra. "Then we all got split up."

"There's not as much for kids our age to do anymore," Sarah added. "And there are only sixty-two kids in our class. So many of us have left the island. But there are fewer cliques—we're all friends. And the divisions between big people and teens aren't obvious now—the boundary line between adulthood and teens doesn't exist anymore. It makes us more responsible."

"If the volcano hadn't happened," Simorra said, "we'd have more opportunities here on the island for when we're older. We wouldn't have to leave to go to college."

But both girls feel the volcano has made them stronger. "I've learned not to take anything for granted," said Sarah, "to take pride in what we have but to always know that nothing lasts forever, so you have to cherish what you have. You learn how to move forward. And most times, the only thing you can take with you is what you've learned, what you have on the inside."

catered:
supplied what was needed or wanted.

CHIEF MINISTER LOWELL LEWIS'S AND DAVID LEA'S STORIES

Dr. Lowell Lewis gave up a successful practice as a kidney transplant specialist in England to become Montserrat's chief minister. David Lea came to Montserrat in 1980 as a missionary from the United States; on July 1, 1995, he took a permanent break from his

This little girl was born after the volcano became active; unlike Sarah and Simorra, she does not know what it is like to live without an active volcano as part of her daily reality.

missionary work, never knowing that within a few weeks, he would be completely occupied with a new career: documenting the volcano's activities. Today Dr. Lewis and David are both working hard to rebuild Montserrat. They are passionate about their home, and their ideas for its regrowth are **innovative** and inspiring.

innovative:
the ability to develop new ideas or inventions.

Both men know what it's like to live through a crisis that never ends. David spoke of the twelve years of ashes: ashes in the air, in your mouth, on your pillowcase at night, on your furniture, on your car, a constant reminder of the danger hovering always in the background. Dr. Lewis has a firsthand intimate knowledge of the ways this crisis

Chief Minister Lowell Lewis has big dreams for Montserrat.

David Lea

has affected the people he governs; he is not only their chief minister but their doctor, with one of the few operating clinics on the island. And yet both men also believe that in the midst of this long crisis is the **potential** for both healing and new opportunities.

As Arthur Meade said, the volcano lives with the islanders—and now they have to learn to live with it. Both David and Dr.

Lewis believe that the very thing that has brought so much destruction and hardship to the island—the volcano—may ultimately hold the answers for the island's regrowth. The volcano now offers the islanders hope.

Geothermal energy is the biggest source of this hope. If the island could develop the technology to harvest this bountiful source of clean energy, Montserrat could not only become completely self-sufficient from an energy perspective, but it could also provide cheap, clean energy to the rest of the Caribbean Islands. What's more, the island has an unlimited supply of wind, solar, and wave energy. David and Dr. Lewis dream that the island could become a center for alternative energy, a place where even the cars don't run on gas, a role model for the rest of the world.

What Is Geothermal Energy?

It's energy generated by heat stored beneath the Earth's surface, and it offers a number of advantages over fossil fuel sources (like oil). From an environmental standpoint, the energy harnessed is clean and safe for the surrounding environment. It is also sustainable because the hot water used in the geothermal process can be put back into the ground to produce more steam. Even better, geothermal power plants are unaffected by changing weather conditions, and they can work continually, day and night.

NO
SMOKING
WITHIN
50 FEET
OF AIRCRAFT

David Lea with some of the rocks that regularly fall on Montserrat. These are not even particularly big stones—much bigger ones have been known to fall from the sky!

Volcano tourism could also bring jobs, money, and regrowth to the island. Montserrat's buried capital city of Plymouth is a modern-day Pompeii; the island's volcano observatory offers fascinating, up-close views of an active volcano; and the island's many trails are lush and beautiful. Before the volcano, Montserrat was on the fast track toward major development as a tourist attraction, but the volcano put a stop to that. Both Dr. Lewis and David Lea want to accept the gift the volcano offers the island now for a different kind of development.

With no port (due to volcanic material filling up the old harbor) and a small airport (where only "puddle-jumper" planes can land because the original airport was destroyed by the volcano in 1997), tourists have a difficult time finding their way to Montserrat. Dr. Lewis wants to rebuild both the port and the airport—but not to the point that Montserrat

What Is Pompeii?

Pompeii was once a thriving city near modern Naples in Italy. But in 79 CE it was completely buried in ash and pumice, during a catastrophic volcanic eruption of Mount Vesuvius. For nearly 1700 years, the city was lost, but in 1748, its ruins were discovered, preserved beneath the layers of volcanic material. Since then, the ruins' ongoing excavation has provided archeologists with amazing insights into what life was like at the height of the Roman Empire. Today, Pompeii is one of Italy's most popular tourist attractions.

Small airplanes like this one are the only ones that can land on Montserrat's airstrip.

would become vulnerable to a destructive onslaught of tourism development. Smaller facilities—a harbor deep enough for only mid-size cruise ships, a larger airstrip still too small to accommodate jets—would limit how many people could come to Montserrat at once. Dr. Lewis wants to attract the sort of tourist who will appreciate the island's true gifts: honeymooners who will enjoy the romance of a peaceful stroll through the tranquil privacy of Montserrat's trails more

Volcanoes and the Gods

Our word "volcano" comes from the name of a god. According to Roman mythology, Vulcan, the god of fire, hammered on his fiery forge deep in the bowels of the Earth, shaping the weapons of the gods. He lived beneath Mount Etna (a volcano that is still active today), and the fire from his forge was sometimes so great that it leapt out from the mountaintop, destroying nearby villages.

Many other cultures have also considered volcanoes to be sacred places, connecting human beings with the world of the gods. Japan's greatest volcano, Mount Fujiyama, is the kingdom of the sun god; El Misti in Peru is inhabited by a god whose wrath sometimes spills out across the inhabitants of the surrounding land; the Native people of the Pacific Northwest believed that the fire god lived in Mount Mazama, while the snow god had his dwelling place in Mount Shasta (Crater Lake, which lies between the two mountains, was created, according to legend, in a battle between the two gods). The goddess Pelé still makes her presence known to Hawaiians by means of the many volcanoes throughout the Hawaiian Islands.

Sometimes, the people of the world have seen volcanic eruptions as being divine punishment on human beings. In 1600, when a volcano erupted in Peru, the Spaniards believed God was punishing them for their sins; unmarried couples who were living together got married, and debtors settled their accounts. Two centuries later, when a volcano erupted in San Salvador, the survivors believed the goddess of the volcano was angry because a boat was doing business on a nearby lake that belonged to her. An 1886 volcano in New Zealand, which buried three villages and killed more than a hundred people, was considered to be the gods' punishment on the villagers for associating with Europeans.

In Montserrat, the contrast between a living Earth and a wasted, barren Earth are side by side. Here, the sides of the volcano reveal the shadowy ghosts of trees and what were once people's homes.

Wisdom from an Ancient Roman Volcano Survivor

"Lava-stone . . . claims [Mount] Etna for its own. . . . Every other substance dies after it has been lighted: Nothing remains therein to be recovered—merely ashes and earth with not a seed of flame. But this lava-stone, submissive time and again, after absorbing a thousand fires, renews its strength."

ecotourists: travelers who visit natural areas with the goal of reducing environmental impact.

microcosm: a small community that is an example of a much larger unit; a little world.

macrocosm: a unit that is a larger example of one of its components; the whole world.

than they would the posh luxury of a five-star resort; students who want to study the volcano or alternative energy; **ecotourists** who will appreciate the island's unspoiled beauty and friendliness.

Both Dr. Lewis and David Lea have hopes that are pinned on practical possibilities. But they cannot accomplish their dreams without the help of others. Ultimately, Earth's entire community must work together in order to make dreams like theirs come true.

In many ways, Montserrat is a **microcosm**, a tiny version of the entire Earth's **macrocosm**. Like so many of Earth's inhabitants, the people of Montserrat face Nature's wrath in real and practical ways that affect their everyday lives. Their only hope of surmounting these challenges is by learning to work with Nature, to respect its power while creating ways to harvest its bounty.

Hurricanes, tsunamis, and volcanoes remind us that the Earth is alive and often

A Survivor of the Eruption of Mount Vesuvius in 79 CE

In the first century, the Roman author, Pliny the Younger, wrote about the death of his uncle, Pliny the Elder, during the eruption of Mount Vesuvius. "My uncle, true savant that he was, deemed the phenomenon important and worth a nearer view. . . . Hastening to the place from whence others were flying, he steered his direct course to the point of danger, with such freedom from fear. . . . And now cinders, which grew thicker and hotter the nearer he approached, fell onto the ships, then pumice-stones too, with stones blackened, scorched, and cracked by fire, the sea ebbed suddenly from under them, while the shore was blocked up by the landslips from the mountains. . . . In the meanwhile Mount Vesuvius was blazing in several places with spreading and towering flames. . . . It was now day everywhere else, but there a deeper darkness prevailed than in the most obscure night. . . . A strong smell of sulphur . . . dispersed the rest of the company in flight, [my uncle] fell; some unusually gross vapour, as I conjecture, having obstructed his breathing and blocked his windpipe, which was naturally weak and chronically inflamed. . . . His body was found entire and uninjured. . . ; its posture was that of a sleeping rather than a dead man."

dangerous, that we cannot take it for granted. But these are short-term events (even when they last twelve years!) compared to the reality we are facing today. Global warming is the ultimate expression of Nature's wrath, and it is a phenomenon that will not go away quickly or easily. Just as the people of Montserrat face both opportunities and dangers, so do we all. The final outcome—for both Montserrat and our entire planet—is still uncertain.

The Earth's Mysteries

Blaming God (or the gods) for volcanic activity was one way our ancestors tried to make sense of the Earth's mysterious forces. But other early thinkers searched for more "scientific" explanations. For instance, Empedocles, a Greek philosopher who lived in the fifth century before the common era, decided that the world is ruled by four elements, "the roots of all things": water, air, earth, and underground fire (which escaped through volcanoes). He himself was a volcano survivor who witnessed Mount Etna's eruption. He wrote, "Masses of fire advance . . . they roll pell-mell shapeless pieces of rock, clouds of black sand fly up with a crash. . . . Nothing can stop the fiery surge, no dam could contain it." Aristotle, who lived about a century later than Empedocles, believed that the Earth is a living organism that is born, lives, and dies. He believed that volcanoes were convulsions caused by the Earth's bouts of fever.

The Account of a Sixteenth-Century Volcano Survivor

"On the 27th and 28th of last September, earth tremors were felt continually, night and day, in the town of Pozzouli [in Italy]. . . . On the 29th, the earth opened near the lake and presented an awful mouth which furiously vomited smoke, fire, stones. . . . The stones were turned to pumice by the devouring flames, and the size of some of them exceeded that of an ox."
—*Pietro Giacomo de Toledo, 1539*

The Account of an Eighteenth-Century Volcano Survivor

"I heard a violent noise within the mountain [Vesuvius], and at about a quarter of a mile off the place where I stood, the mountain split and with much noise, from this new mouth a fountain of liquid shot up many feet high, and then like a torrent, rolled on directly toward us. The earth shook at the same time that a volley of pumice stones fell thick upon us; in an instant clouds of black and ashes caused an almost total darkness; the explosions from the top of the mountain were much louder than any thunder I have ever heard, and the smell of the sulphur was very offensive. My guide alarmed took to his heels, and I must confess that I was not at my ease. I followed close, and we ran near three miles without stopping. . . . After having taken breath, as the earth still trembled greatly, I thought it most prudent to leave the mountain."
—*Sir William Hamilton, 1776*

Chapter Five

GLOBAL WARMING: *BEING A SURVIVOR ON PLANET EARTH*

Many natural disasters are unavoidable; as tragic as they are for human life, they are simply part of the Earth's normal geologic and climatic patterns. Sometimes, however, human activities have either intensified these patterns or done away with the natural protections that once existed (as was the case along America's Gulf Region, where so many wetlands have been destroyed). Today, human beings are facing the most long-term and widespread natural disaster our planet may have encountered since the catastrophe that put an end to the dinosaurs: global warming.

Although scientists and politicians continue to argue over just how bad the problem is, some facts are clear: CO_2 emissions from our cars, homes, and factories have turned our

Extreme Weather and Global Warming

When the Earth's average temperature rises, more heat energy goes into the atmosphere, while at the same time the warmer air can hold greater amounts of water vapor. This combination fuels heavier rainfalls, more frequent heat waves (which increase the risk of drought), and fiercer windstorms (including hurricanes, tornadoes, and typhoons). Scientists say that computer models predict that even wilder weather lies ahead.

Arctic habitats are some of the most vulnerable to the effects of global warming. As the ice shelves shrink, polar bears often drown because they are unable to swim the increasing distances between land and the receding ice.

planet into a greenhouse that traps the sun's heat inside our atmosphere. As a result, the Earth is on average 1.3°F (0.7°C) warmer today than it was a hundred years ago. This may not seem like enough to worry about—but even tiny changes in temperature can affect weather patterns, as well as the ability of certain species to survive. The most dramatic changes in the Earth's temperature have occurred in the Arctic, where in the past fifty years, as the thermometer has risen on average by 4° to 5°F (2.2° to 2.8°C), the polar ice cap is rapidly melting.

As Aristotle would have said centuries ago, the Earth has a temperature. Mother Earth is sick with a fever, a fever caused by her children's actions. Her illness will ultimately affect us all. Meanwhile, around the globe, human life is already being affected.

TUVALU

In the Pacific Ocean is another island nation, a little like Montserrat. But in this case, it's not a volcano that threatens the people of Tuvalu. They face a far greater threat: the total loss of their island home. The islands that make up Tuvalu are only three feet above sea level—and as global warming makes the sea rise, this tiny nation is expected to eventually disappear beneath the water forever.

Many Tuvalans are already leaving their islands, moving their communities to higher ground in West Auckland, New Zealand.

The small Polynesian island of Tuvalu is threatened by the rising sea.

taro:
a large-leaved plant grown throughout the tropics for its edible, potato-like corm (an underground stem base similar to a bulb).

Western:
characteristic of the culture of countries in America and Western Europe.

It's a very different world there: no coconut trees, no **taro** plants, only streets and malls and modern **Western** life.

Peni Taniela is one of the Tuvalan refugees who now lives in New Zealand. As a teenager, he heard that some day the sea would rise and drown his island, but back then he never gave it much thought. "My dad said, 'Oh, don't worry about that.'" But on Tuvalu the high tides became higher; beaches grew smaller; and the soil became wetter.

Like the Moken sea gypsies, the Tuvalans face not only the loss of their physical home;

they also face the loss of their cultural identity. Peni's father said, "When I was young I was told that there are two main things you have to learn if you want to live in Tuvalu: how to climb the coconut tree and how to fish. If you know these two then you will live. But in New Zealand, no, you have to have an income. It's a very challenging place. Everything you do, it costs you money."

Another Tuvalan, Fala Aulangi, said, "What really concerns me is that at the end of the day [people will say], 'Hey, where are you from? Which island?' And I'll say, 'Oh, I'm from Tuvalu.' They'll say, 'And where is that?' What shall I say, 'Oh, it has disappeared or submerged under the sea because of global warming?' So, like that's our identity, our culture. Everything will disappear. We may get together here as a community and celebrate when it's Independence Day,

What Do the Scientists Say?

Not all scientists agree that global warming will cause low-lying land to be submerged beneath rising oceans. The Intergovernmental Panel on Climate Change, however, which represents the consensus of 2,000 scientists, predicts that over the next fifty to a hundred years global warming will cause oceans to rise as much as three feet and possibly much higher, depending on the melting of the Antarctic and Greenland ice sheets. Tuvalu and other islands that are low-lying and narrow are particularly vulnerable.

our successes and things, but it's different. Definitely, it's going to be really hard for us to accept that we're no longer on the map. And it's no joke."

LAKE TANGANYIKA, TANZANIA

Lake Tanganyika is home to thousands of creatures, including humans who depend on it for their livelihoods.

Africa's Lake Tanganyika, the longest fresh water lake in the world and the second deepest, provides homes and food for a variety of living creatures, including human beings, who rely on the lake's fish for sustenance. Many of Tanganyika's 350 species of fish live nowhere else on Earth, because the lake offers a unique

ecosystem: up until recently, its temperature has been almost **uniformly** consistent, even in its deepest water, 4,700 feet down. Unfortunately, global warming may be affecting Lake Tanganyika. Even a few degrees difference in temperature kills fish—and affects the livelihoods of millions of people.

Seph, a fisherman on Lake Tanganyika, said that fishing is much more difficult now than it was thirty years ago when he was a teenager. "Oh, it was so good," he said. "When we used to fish with our fathers, it was really good. There were so many dagaa [a type of sardine]. People could fish five thousand tons. In tons! Back in those days there was so much dagaa."

Like the fishing communities of America's Gulf region and Thailand's Indian Ocean, the people who live on Lake Tanganyika's shore rely on Nature for their livelihoods. Seph said, "We fish because we have no other job. Our grandfathers fished here. Our fathers fished here. We'll fish here and pass it on to our children who will fish and pass it on again. It's our **legacy**."

If the fish disappear, what legacy will Seph—and the fishers of other waters around the world—leave to their children?

MOUNT KILIMANJARO, TANZANIA

The effects of global warming are being felt in another region of Tanzania as well: on the

ecosystem: a community of livings things and their environment interacting and functioning as an ecological unit.

uniformly: unvarying; keeping the same form.

legacy: something passed on to the next generation by an ancestor or from the past.

slopes of Mount Kilimanjaro, Africa's tallest mountain, which rises 20,000 feet above a dry **savanna** in northern Tanzania. The snowfields on the mountain are slowly shrinking; scientists say they will vanish completely in the next ten to fifteen years.

Mount Kilimanjaro is a name of romance and **mystique**; the loss of its snow is an **aesthetic** loss to the entire world. But as always, human life cannot be separated from the Earth's. The people who rely on melting snow for their water are also at risk.

William Kiwali, chairman of the small village in Tanzania, said, "I'm a farmer. I grow coffee, corn, and bananas. . . . My farm is dry now, and so are the other farms, because there is not enough water. . . . In the past there was a lot of ice on the mountain, and the rivers were so full we could not cross them. Now there's not enough water and the ice is diminished . . . a lot of ditches are dried out and the rivers are low. And even the rivers that have water only have a little."

These losses bring about changes in human society as well. "There's not enough water for people," Mr. Kiwali said, "so they start quarreling. Sometimes they cut each other with machetes. It's not normal. In the past there was no such thing."

NATIVE PEOPLE PROTECTING THE EARTH

The first people to notice—and speak out against—global warming have often been

The snow fields on Mt. Kilimanjaro are shrinking because of global warming.

tribal groups. People like Peni, Seph, and William Kiwali live more closely to the Earth than most of the modern world; their lives are the first to change when the Earth changes, and they are the first survivors of global warming. It's not surprising then, that some of clearest voices speaking out on this issue come from Native **activists** and scientists.

SHEILA WATT-CLOUTIER

Sheila Watt-Cloutier is an **Inuit** scientist and activist who has been warning the world about the dangers of global warming. Along with

activists: people who fight strongly for or against a controversial issue.

Inuit: the group of culturally similar native peoples inhabiting the Arctic regions of North America, Greenland, and Russia.

Sheila Watt-Cloutier

former U.S. vice president Al Gore, she was nominated for a Nobel Peace Prize for her work to bring this issue to the world's attention. (Ultimately, only Mr. Gore was granted the prize, though the Nobel committee never explained why.) Today she is the elected chairperson of the Inuit Circumpolar Conference, which represents the 155,000 Inuit who live in Alaska, Canada, Greenland, and Chukotka, Russia. She sees global warming as the biggest danger facing her people. She wrote in the U.K. *Guardian*:

While global warming is affecting the entire planet, there is a scientific consensus that it is impacting the Arctic much faster. Our elders and hunters have intimate knowledge of the land and sea ice, and have observed disturbing changes to the Arctic climate and environment, and to the wildlife. These changes include melting **permafrost** causing increased erosion and damaging **infrastructure**; longer sea-ice free seasons; new species of birds and fish invading the region; the arrival of mosquitoes and blackflies; unpredictable sea-ice conditions; and glaciers melting fast, creating torrents instead of streams.

My homeland, the Arctic, is the health barometer for the planet. By

permafrost:
a permanently frozen layer of ground found at different levels in the colder regions of the planet.

infrastructure:
the system of public works (roads, bridges, water supply, etc...) of a country, state, or city.

looking at what is already happening in remote Inuit villages in Alaska, such as Shismaref and Kivalina, you can understand the dangers for more populated areas of the world. Scientists tell us that polar bears, ice living seals, walrus, and some birds are very likely to decline, and that warming will disrupt or destroy our hunting and food sharing culture. Our ancient connection to our hunting culture may well disappear, within my grandson's lifetime. My culture continues to see us through much tumultuous change. This change has resulted in confusion and despair, and all too often in early death for our young people from suicides and addiction.

Climate change is a matter of the survival of humanity as whole. It is the most pressing global issue we face today. Protect the Arctic and we will save the planet.

WINONA LaDUKE

Winona LaDuke is another Native activist whose voice is one of the clearest speaking out on behalf of our planet. She wrote:

Native American teachings describe the relations all around—animals, fish, trees, and rocks—as our brothers, sisters, uncles, and grandpas. Our relations

Winona LaDuke

to each other, our prayers whispered across generations to our relatives, are what bind our cultures together. . . .

Their absence may mean that a people sing to a barren river, a caged bear, or a buffalo far away. It is the struggle to preserve what remains and the struggle to recover what has been lost that characterizes much of Native environmentalism. It is these relationships that **industrialism** seeks to disrupt. Native communities will resist with great determination.

PATAKA MOORE

Pataka Moore is a Maori scientist in New Zealand; like LaDuke, he recognizes the importance of the Earth's health to human culture. He said:

As tribal groups we relate not only to this country, but we relate specifically to places in this country. Places that are sacred to us that have *mana*, that have *maori*, that have *whe*, that have *ihe*, that have *tapu*. If we're to lose some of these key components of what makes us us, elements of our culture, I mean, once that's lost, what do we become?

WHAT CAN YOU DO?

Native activists may be among the first and loudest voices to speak out on behalf of the Earth, but today other voices have joined theirs. As citizens of the modern world, we may not see as clearly as tribal groups do our intimate connections to our planet—but those connections are still real and necessary to our well-being. Without them, we will die. As more and more people recognize this, more and more of us are taking steps to change the way we live. If we want human beings to survive, we have to!

> ## Energy Fact
>
> The average North American family sends about 50,000 pounds of CO_2 into the atmosphere a year. (That's 19 times more per capita than the average family in India does.) About half that CO_2 comes from our homes, the other half from our cars and other vehicles.

As *Life* author Peter Miller wrote, "Climate change isn't just about smokestacks and melting glaciers. It's also about individuals like you and me. We play a bigger role in changing the Earth's climate than you might think, and we can be a part of the solution as well."

Here are some of the things we can all do to help protect the Earth:

- Cut back on air conditioning use. (Use fans instead, which use 98 percent less energy.)
- Use cooler water for showers and laundry.

- Replace light bulbs with compact fluorescent bulbs (which use 75 percent less energy than incandescent bulbs).
- Turn off lights, appliances, and other electric items when they're not in use.
- Plug televisions, computers, cable boxes, printers, video game players, battery chargers, and all other such devices into a power strip that can be turned off when not in use. (Otherwise, these things continue to suck power even when they're not "on.")
- Ride a bike or walk instead of taking the car whenever possible.
- Decrease vacations that require air flight; look for things to do and places to explore that are closer to home.
- Use local produce and meats. (Transporting these items from across the country or around the world has a hefty cost in terms of CO_2 emissions.)

As the survivors of the tsunami, Hurricane Katrina, and the Montserrat volcano have all learned, even in the face of a disaster, there is hope. The answer lies in our ability to work together, to unite as a community, in this case, a global community, where everyone—scientists, politicians, business owners, homeowners, children—work together. Together we have to learn new habits, create new lifestyles, ones that aren't dependent on gas and oil. There is no going back to "normal life." As so many survivors of natural disasters have learned, it's time to build a "new normal." We need to do this for our mother, our planet—and we need to do it for each other. Bottom line: We need to do it for ourselves.

What Do Survivors Know?

Laurence Gonzales, author of the book *Deep Survival*, says that all survivors of natural disasters have learned some of the same things. Here's a list of a few of those things that can be applied to the planet's current challenge:

- See the problem; don't deny that it's real.
- Don't let fear rule you; instead, use your anger to give you energy.
- Analyze the situation and make a plan.
- Take action!
- Celebrate even small successes.
- Reach out to others; don't focus only on yourself.
- Enjoy the journey. Take time to laugh, to appreciate the Earth's beauty, to find pleasure in daily life.
- Believe that you will succeed.
- Do whatever is necessary.
- Never give up.

Further Reading

Knauer, Kelly, ed. *Global Warming*. New York, N.Y.: Time, 2007.

Kolbert, Elizabeth. *Field Notes from a Catastrophe: Man, Nature, and Climate Change.* New York, N.Y.: Bloomsbury USA, 2007.

Krafft, Maurice. *Volcanoes: Fire from the Earth.* New York, N.Y.: Abrams, 2007.

Life Books. *Nature's Fury: Wild Weather & Natural Disasters.* New York, N.Y.: Life, 2008.

Lovelock, James. *The Revenge of Gaia: Earth's Climate Crisis & the Fate of Humanity.* New York, N.Y.: Basic Books, 2006.

McKibben, Bill. *Hope, Human and Wild: True Stories of Living Lightly on the Earth.* Boston, MA: Milkweed Editions, 1995.

Sanna, Ellyn. *The Gift of Hope: In the Wake of the 2004 Tsunami and the 2005 Hurricanes.* Vestal, N.Y.: Village Earth Books, 2006.

Steffen, Alex. *World Changing: A User's Guide for the 21st Century.* New York, N.Y.: Abrams, Inc., 2006.

For More Information

American Red Cross
www.redcross.org
Deals with helping communities and victims affected by disasters. Provides opportunities to volunteer or donate to those in need.

Disaster Action
www.disasteraction.org.uk/support/
  da_guide07.htm
This Web site is to help survivors of disasters and the families of those who died. Provides ways to support others, information on Post Traumatic Stress Disorder (PTSD), and a variety of helpful links.

EPA: United States Environmental Protection Agency
www.epa.gov/epahome/learn.htm
Government-run agency to protect the environment and help prevent any pollution or global warming. Leads the environmental research and education in the United States.

FEMA
http://www.fema.gov/index.shtm
Web site for the Federal Emergency Management Agency (FEMA), a government run agency created for the purpose of helping those who have suffered as a result of natural disasters or terrorist activities. Contains information on different types of disaster and ways to plan ahead.

How Volcanoes Work
www.geology.sdsu.edu/how_volcanoes_work
This Web site includes educational info on the science of volcanoes and their eruptions.

For More Information

Hurricane Preparedness
www.nhc.noaa.gov/HAW2/english/basics.
  shtml
This informational Web site covers a variety of hurricane-based topics, including basic facts, how to be prepared, what to do in case of flooding or high winds, and information on tornadoes.

NOAA Center for Tsunami Research
nctr.pmel.noaa.gov
Center of research concerning tsunamis. Includes forecasting, past tsunami events, and basic frequently asked questions concerning the topic.

"Price of Paradise" Volcano DVD Series
www.priceofparadise.com
Web site for the video journal produced by David Lea, of the volcano that erupted on the Caribbean Island of Montserrat.

Publisher's note:
The Web sites listed on these pages were active at the time of publication. The publisher is not responsible for Web sites that have changed their addresses or discontinued operation since the date of publication. The publisher will review and update the Web-site list upon each reprint.

Bibliography

Costanza, R., L. J. Graumlich, and W. Steffen, eds. *Sustainability or Collapse? An Integrated History and Future of People on Earth.* Dahlem Workshop Report 96. Cambridge, Mass.: MIT Press, 2007.

Diamond. J. *Collapse: How Societies Choose to Fail or Succeed.* New York, N.Y.: Viking, 2005.

"Early Signs: Reports from a Warming Planet." Living on Earth, www.loe.org/series/early-signs.htm.

Hornborg, A., J. R. McNeill, and J. Martinez-Alier. *Rethinking Environmental History: World-System History and Global Environmental Change.* Lanham, Md.: Altamira Press, 2007.

Krafft, Maurice. *Volcanoes: Fire from the Earth.* New York, N.Y.: Abrams, 2007.

LaDuke, Winona. *All Our Relations: Native Struggles for Land and Life.* Cambridge, Mass.: Brookline, 2001.

Life Books. *Nature's Fury: Wild Weather & Natural Disasters.* New York, N.Y.: Life, 2008.

National Geographic. Special Report: Changing Climate, June 22, 2008.

Redman, C. L., S. R. James, P. R. Fish, and J. D. Rogers. *The Archaeology of Global Change: The Impact of Humans on Their Environment.* Washington, D.C.: Smithsonian Books, 2004.

Index

Picture Credits

American Red Cross: p. 30-31

Andrews, Benjamin E.: p. 21

Centre for Native Policy and Research: p. 116

Dheva-aksorn, Boonsruong: p. 32

Dreamstime
    1911guy: p. 107
    Boiteau, Daniel: p. 112
    Clay-Ballard, Laura: p. 18-19
    Dusanzidar: p. 9
    Fouquin, Christophe: p. 28
    Grondin, Julien: p. 74
    Leaf: p. 8
    Lyngfjell, Geir-olav: p. 12-13
    Outdoorsman: p. 112
    Ravbar, Uros: p. 26

Harding House Publishing
    Stewart, Benjamin: p. 35, 37, 38-39, 42, 44, 46-47, 50, 51, 52-53, 54, 64, 65, 67, 69, 71, 72, 78, 80, 81, 83, 85, 86, 87, 89, 91, 92-93, 94, 96, 98, 100-101

NASA: p. 58, 60

National Science Foundation
    Andrew Cohen: p. 110

Schinkel, Mike: p. 76

U.S. Department of Agriculture: p. 24-25

U.S. National Archives and Records Administration: p. 22-23

Wikipedia
    Jastrow: p. 14

Winona LaDuke: p. 118

The Yorck Project
    Hayez, Francisco: p. 16

About the Author and the Consultant

Author

Ellyn Sanna is the author of many books. She has worked as a social worker, a teacher, an editor, and a small-business owner. She lives in New York State with her family, a couple of dogs, several goats, and a cat.

Consultant

Andrew M. Kleiman, M.D. is a Clinical Instructor in Psychiatry at New York University School of Medicine. He received a BA in philosophy from the University of Michigan, and graduated from Tulane University School of Medicine. Dr. Kleiman completed his internship, residency, and fellowship in psychiatry at New York University and Bellevue Hospital. He is currently in private practice in Manhattan and teaches at New York University School of Medicine.